Walker

by Iain Gray

LangSyne
PUBLISHING
WRITING *to* REMEMBER

LangSyne
PUBLISHING
WRITING *to* REMEMBER

79 Main Street, Newtongrange,
Midlothian EH22 4NA
Tel: 0131 344 0414   Fax: 0845 075 6085
E-mail: info@lang-syne.co.uk
www.langsyneshop.co.uk

Design by Dorothy Meikle
Printed by Printwell Ltd
© Lang Syne Publishers Ltd 2017

ISBN 978-1-85217-210-7

Walker

MOTTO:
How Great are Honourable Deeds.

*The spirit of the clan means
much to thousands of people*

Chapter one:

Origins of Scottish surnames

by George Forbes

It all began with the Normans.

For it was they who introduced surnames into common usage more than a thousand years ago, initially based on the title of their estates, local villages and chateaux in France to distinguish and identify these landholdings, usually acquired at the point of a bloodstained sword.

Such grand descriptions also helped enhance the prestige of these arrogant warlords and generally glorify their lofty positions high above the humble serfs slaving away below in the pecking order who only had single names, often with Biblical connotations as in Pierre and Jacques.

The only descriptive distinctions among this peasantry concerned their occupations, like Pierre the swineherd or Jacques the ferryman.

The Normans themselves were originally Vikings (or Northmen) who raided, colonised and eventually settled down around the French coastline.

They had sailed up the Seine in their longboats in 900AD under their ferocious leader Rollo and ruled the roost in north east France before sailing over to conquer England, bringing their relatively new tradition of having surnames with them.

It took another hundred years for the Normans to percolate northwards and surnames did not begin to appear in Scotland until the thirteenth century.

These adventurous knights brought an aura of chivalry with them and it was said no damsel of any distinction would marry a man unless he had at least two names.

The family names included that of Scotland's great hero Robert De Brus and his compatriots were warriors from families like the De Morevils, De Umphravils, De Berkelais, De Quincis, De Viponts and De Vaux.

As the knights settled the boundaries of their vast estates, they took territorial names, as in Hamilton, Moray, Crawford, Cunningham, Dunbar, Ross, Wemyss, Dundas, Galloway, Renfrew, Greenhill, Hazelwood, Sandylands and Church-hill.

Other names, though not with any obvious geographical or topographical features, nevertheless derived from ancient parishes like Douglas, Forbes, Dalyell and Guthrie.

Other surnames were coined in connection with occupations, castles or legendary deeds.

Stuart originated in the word steward, a prestigious post which was an integral part of any large medieval household. The same applied to Cooks, Chamberlains, Constables and Porters.

Borders towns and forts – needed in areas like the Debateable Lands which were constantly fought over by feuding local families – had their own distinctive names; and it was often from them that the resident groups took their communal titles, as in the Grahams of Annandale, the Elliots and Armstrongs of the East Marches, the Scotts and Kerrs of Teviotdale and Eskdale.

Even physical attributes crept into surnames, as in Small, Little and More (the latter being 'beg' in Gaelic), Long or Lang, Stark, Stout, Strong or Strang and even Jolly.

Mieklejohns would have had the strength of several men, while Littlejohn was named after the legendary sidekick of Robin Hood.

Colours got into the act with Black, White, Grey, Brown and Green (Red developed into Reid, Ruddy or Ruddiman). Blue was rare and nobody ever wanted to be associated with yellow.

Pompous worthies took the name Wiseman, Goodman and Goodall.

Words intimating the sons of leading figures were soon affiliated into the language as in Johnson, Adamson, Richardson and Thomson, while the Norman equivalent of Fitz (from the French-Latin 'filius' meaning 'son') cropped up in Fitzmaurice and Fitzgerald.

The prefix 'Mac' was 'son of' in Gaelic and clans often originated with occupations – as in

MacNab being sons of the Abbot, MacPherson and MacVicar being sons of the minister and MacIntosh being sons of the chief.

The church's influence could be found in the names Kirk, Clerk, Clarke, Bishop, Friar and Monk. Proctor came from a church official, Singer and Sangster from choristers, Gilchrist and Gillies from Christ's servant, Mitchell, Gilmory and Gilmour from servants of St Michael and Mary, Malcolm from a servant of Columba and Gillespie from a bishop's servant.

The rudimentary medical profession was represented by Barber (a trade which also once included dentistry and surgery) as well as Leech or Leitch.

Businessmen produced Merchants, Mercers, Monypennies, Chapmans, Sellers and Scales, while down at the old village watermill the names that cropped up included Miller, Walker and Fuller.

Other self explanatory trades included Coopers, Brands, Barkers, Tanners, Skinners, Brewsters and Brewers, Tailors, Saddlers, Wrights,

Cartwrights, Smiths, Harpers, Joiners, Sawyers, Masons and Plumbers.

Even the scenery was utilised as in Craig, Moor, Hill, Glen, Wood and Forrest.

Rank, whether high or low, took its place with Laird, Barron, Knight, Tennant, Farmer, Husband, Granger, Grieve, Shepherd, Shearer and Fletcher.

The hunt and the chase supplied Hunter, Falconer, Fowler, Fox, Forrester, Archer and Spearman.

The renowned medieval historian Froissart, who eulogised about the romantic deeds of chivalry (and who condemned Scotland as being a poverty stricken wasteland), once sniffily dismissed the peasantry of his native France as the jacquerie (or the jacques-without-names) but it was these same humble folk who ended up overthrowing the arrogant aristocracy.

In the olden days, only the blueblooded knights of antiquity were entitled to full, proper names, both Christian and surnames, but with the passing of time and a more egalitarian, less feudal atmosphere, more respectful and worthy titles spread throughout the populace as a whole.

Echoes of a far distant past can still be found in most names and they can be borne with pride in commemoration of past generations who fought and toiled in some capacity or other to make our nation what it now is, for good or ill.

Chapter two:

Kindred of the clans

The surname Walker, in all its rich and often confusing variety of spellings, originally denoted someone whose skills were vital to the wider community: this was the trade of fulling, the working of woven cloth to a thickness that would allow the tailoring of garments.

The process was known as 'waulking', and involved the repeated kneading of cloth, either by hand or by trampling it underfoot, until the required thickness was achieved.

Waulking was carried out for many centuries by the women of remote highland and island communities to the haunting rhythm of what were known as waulking songs, and these songs remain an integral part of the colourful Gaelic musical tradition.

The root of today's 'Walker' is from the Old English 'Wealcere', and varieties of spelling throughout the centuries have included

Walcair, Walcar, Walcare, Walkar, Walkster, Waulcar, and, particularly in Scotland, Waulker.

Gaelic equivalents found in Scotland all derive from Mac an Fhucadar, meaning 'son of the fuller'. These forms include MacNucator, MacNuccator, McNowcatter, and MacNucatter, and many of these 'sons of the fuller' plied their trades as important members of the community of clans.

This means that some of today's Walkers scattered across the globe may well be descendants of these original Gaelic speaking 'sons of the fuller', and we will find how they can claim allegiance to two clans in particular: the proud MacMillans and the Stewarts of Appin.

Both these Walkers of the Highlands and Islands and their counterparts in the Scottish Lowlands were to play a significant role in the high romance and drama of Scotland's story, while in later years Walkers would gain fame, and in some cases infamy, in a wide variety of pursuits.

'Walkers', in various spellings of the name, appear in Scottish records from as early as 1324, a mere ten years after the decisive battle of Bannockburn and four years after the signing of that ringing endorsement of Scotland's right to freedom and independence known as the Declaration of Arbroath.

It is in 1324 that a Thomas Walker is recorded in Berwickshire, while a John Walker is recorded in Elgin in 1393. A Donald Walcare appears on record in Edinburgh in 1457, and this is forty-three years before a Craft of Waulkers was founded in the town, giving an indication of the importance of the skill.

It is in the vast and sprawling territory of Argyll that the connection between the Walkers and Clan MacMillan is to be found, a connection so strong that Walker is one of the 'names' officially associated with the clan.

A Donald Roye McInocador appears at Knapdale, in Argyll, in 1547 and a Martino McNowcatter at Inveraray in 1647; Patrick McNowcatter was serving in the powerful and prestigious post of procurator fiscal for Argyll in 1655, while a Donald Walker is recorded at Inveraray in 1699.

A hand brandishing a sword is the crest and 'I learn to succour the distressed' is the motto of Clan MacMillan, the name deriving from the Gaelic Mhaolian, meaning 'tonsured', and this indicates that the ancestors of the clan were a family of priests who, in all probability, traced their origins back to Ireland.

Whatever their origins, these 'sons of the tonsured', or MacMillans, are recorded in the twelfth century as settled in lands beside Loch Arkaig, in Lochaber, and later in territory near Loch Tay.

Much of Argyll was held under the powerful sway of the MacDonald Lords of the Isles, who in 1360 confirmed a Malcolm Mor MacMillan in his ownership of lands in Knapdale, in mid-Argyll, and it was here that the MacMillan stronghold of Castle Sween was built.

A grandson of Malcolm, known to

posterity as Lachlan MacMillan of Knap, was slain with hundreds of his clansmen and kinsmen such as the MacNucators (who would later adopt the more familiar English spelling of Walker), in one of the most ferocious clan battles ever fought on Scottish soil.

Known as the battle of Harlaw, or the battle of Red Harlaw, it was fought on July 24, 1411, and was basically a bloody showdown between the wild and unruly clansmen of the west and north of Scotland and their rather more law-abiding neighbours in the lowlands of the northeast.

Donald MacDonald, 2nd Lord of the Isles, had mustered about 6,000 of his most battle-hardened clansmen and kinsmen such as the MacMillans and their kinsmen such as the MacNucators, and torched the town of Inverness after having crossed to the mainland from the MacDonald stronghold of Ardtornish, on the Sound of Mull, and marching up the Great Glen.

His already formidable strength swelled

to 10,000 after other clans (including Chattan, Cameron, Macintosh, and MacLeod) joined him on his destructive progress and, promising them rich plunder, he marched them towards Inverness, where the citizens cowered in terror.

The Earl of Mar, however, hastily assembled a force of northeast lairds and their kinsfolk, while the provost of Aberdeen also raised a citizen militia.

The opposing forces finally met just north of Aberdeen, and battle was joined shortly after the summer sun had risen in the east.

The fearless clansmen repeatedly charged the ranks of Mar's forces, only to be cut down like ripe corn, but not before they had exacted their own dreadful toll in blood: as the sun sank low in the west, both sides were totally exhausted and had to retire from the carnage, leaving behind a battlefield littered with the bodies of at least 1,000 clansmen and 600 of Mar's men.

Aberdeen had been saved, but at a terrible cost to both sides.

As one of the clans that made up the confederacy of clans who owed allegiance to the MacDonald Lords of the Isles, the fortunes of the MacMillans were inextricably linked to those of the MacDonalds.

This was to have dire consequences for the MacMillans and other members of the confederation when, in 1493, with royal authority being flouted at every turn, an exasperated James IV finally annexed the Lordship of the Isles to the Crown.

The resultant power vacuum led to virtual anarchy, with powerful clans such as the Campbells encroaching on territory held by less powerful clans such as the MacMillans and their kinsfolk.

Some MacMillans and kinsfolk such as the MacNucators found a new home much further southwest, in Galloway, while others were forced to flee from Knapdale into Lochaber, where they found themselves tenants of the Macintoshes, who in turn owed allegiance to Clan Cameron.

The originally Gaelic speaking

MacNucators later adopted the English form of 'Walker', and any Walkers of today who can trace ancestry back to those areas of Argyll held by the MacMillans are entitled to claim kinship with the clan and adopt the MacMillan, crest, motto, and tartan.

It is in recognition of the close link between today's Walkers and the MacMillans that a generous supporter for a number of years of the Clan MacMillan Society (of Scotland) has been the family of the world-famous Walkers Shortbread Ltd, founded in 1898 by Joseph Walker and based at Aberlour on Spey, in Banffshire.

Chapter three:

Covenanters and Jacobites

Many of those MacMillans who later found a home in Galloway played a leading role in the bitter seventeenth century struggles between Crown and Covenant, and prominent among these Covenanters was the Reverend John MacMillan, who as late as 1703 was deposed from his practice for his continued opposition to authority.

The Covenanters had taken their name from the National Covenant, first signed in the Greyfriars kirkyard in Edinburgh in February of 1638 in defence of the Presbyterian religion and in opposition to the king's claim of supremacy in matters of religion.

During the Killing Time of 1684 to 1685, hundreds of Covenanters in the south-west of Scotland, such as the MacMillans and their Walker kinsfolk, paid dearly for their stalwart adherence to their faith and their opposition to the Stuart kings.

Ironically, however, other Walkers paid dearly for their adherence to the royal house, and this was through their kinship with the proud Clan Stewart of Appin.

A unicorn's head is the crest and 'Whither will ye' is the motto of Clan Stewart of Appin, the West Highland clan that recognises both MacNucator and Walker as septs, or branches, although not primary septs.

The links are so close, however, that a kinship can be claimed by those Walkers of today who can trace an ancestry back to the Stewart territory of Appin, in Upper Lorn, prior to 1388.

It was in this year that the Stewarts acquired the Lordship of Lorn and, consequently, took into kinship families already settled there such as the MacNucators.

The Appin Stewarts fought at the side of the Royalist John Graham, 1st Marquis of Montrose, during his great campaigns from

1644 to 1645, in support of Charles I and in opposition to the Covenanting authorities.

The Stewarts and their MacNucator kinsmen were present with Montrose on February 2, 1645, when the Earl of Argyll was forced to flee to safety in his galley after 1,500 of his Covenanters were wiped out in a daring surprise attack on Inverlochy.

What made Montrose's victory all the more remarkable was that his hardy forces had arrived at Inverlochy after a gruelling 36-hour march south through knee-deep snow from the area of present-day Fort Augustus.

The Stewarts of Appin also shared in Montrose's victory at Kilsyth on August 15, 1645, but also shared in his final defeat at Philiphaugh, near Selkirk, less than a month later.

Montrose paid for his loyalty to the Stuart cause by being beheaded by the grim instrument of execution known as the Maiden, or guillotine, in Edinburgh five years later, while the Appin estate was forfeited and not restored until the Restoration of Charles II in 1660.

In common with many clans, the Stewarts of Appin attached themselves to what would prove to be the abortive Jacobite Risings of both 1715 and 1745.

In many cases, ordinary clansmen and their kinsmen such as the Walkers had no option but to obey the call of their chief to rally to the standard of the Royal House of Stuart.

Jacobite opposition to the Hanoverian succession of George, Elector of Hanover, in 1714, reached such a pitch that in November of 1715 the Earl of Mar rallied in excess of 10,000 men, including the Appin Stewarts and their kinsmen, to the cause of the exiled James III, known as the Old Pretender.

The cause was effectively lost at the battle of Sheriffmuir in November of that year, however, when Mar withdrew his army north to Perth after engaging the government forces of John Campbell, 2nd Duke of Argyll.

James arrived at Perth later in December, before departing for foreign shores, never again to return.

But the Standard of the exiled Royal House of Stuart was raised once again, when Prince Charles Edward Stuart, known as the Young Pretender, arrived on Scottish shores on August 19, 1745.

Rallying loyal support, a great victory followed at the battle of Prestonpans in September, and a confident Jacobite army left Edinburgh for the march on London at the end of October, only to controversially retire back north in early December after reaching Derby.

It was on April 16, 1746, on Drummossie Moor, near Inverness, that the decisive battle of Culloden was fought, effectively sounding the final death knell of not only the Jacobite cause, but, in the brutal suppression that followed the defeat, a way of life that had endured for centuries.

A number of Walkers are recorded in the muster roll of the Jacobite army of 1745-46: an Alexander Walker, who was captured and tried after Culloden but later released, served with the Forfarshire (Ogilvy's Regiment), while 21-year-old John Walker, a servant, and William Walker from Aberdeen-shire served with Lord Lewis Gordon's Regiment.

A John Walker, described as a labourer from Lancashire, served with the Manchester Regiment, raised by the Jacobites on the abortive march south, while ninety-two Stewart of Appin clansmen are recorded as having been among the many victims of the terrible carnage of Culloden.

While some Walkers fought for the cause of the Royal House of Stuart, others achieved fame for their support of what is known as the Glorious Revolution of 1688 that

brought William of Orange to the throne in favour of James II.

Known to posterity as the Defender of Londonderry, the Reverend George Walker, commissioned as a colonel in the army of William, was killed at the battle of the Boyne in 1690 after going to the aid of Frederic Schomberg, the commander-in-chief of William's forces in Ireland.

Earlier, as governor of Londonderry, he had been instrumental in the city withstanding a 105-day siege by the forces of the deposed James, an event that is commemorated annually.

Following the suppression of the Highland way of life after Culloden, many Highland 'MacNucators' were forced to seek a new life either in the Lowlands or on the far-flung foreign shores of North America, Australia, and New Zealand.

Having adopted the English form of 'Walker', and far from the battlefields, many achieved distinction in a variety of rather more peaceful pursuits.

Raising the standard at Glenfinnan

Chapter four:

Heroes and villains

Sir Walter Scott, who always had an unerring eye for a tale based on real events that he could weave into one of his magnificent fictional creations, is responsible for immortalising a lass from Dumfriesshire known as Helen Walker: as the fictional character Jeanie Deans, she is the heroine of his masterpiece *The Heart of Midlothian*.

The tale on which Scott based his novel concerns Helen Walker and her sister Isabella, who lived at Irongray, about six miles from Dumfries, in the southwest of Scotland.

Isabella was accused of the heinous crime of child murder in 1738, but not murder as it would be considered today: at the time of the events Scott describes, to have a child out of wedlock was viewed as a great sin, and the hapless mother would be virtually ostracised from society.

Many women, understandably, sought to conceal their pregnancy and the subsequent birth of the child, hoping they may have it adopted in secret. But if the infant died in childbirth, as many did, the death was considered a case of murder.

This was the terrible plight Isabella found herself in when she was found guilty of child murder and sentenced to be hanged. Under Scots law, six weeks had to elapse before her execution, and all that could possibly save her was the forlorn hope of a royal pardon.

Her sister Helen accordingly set off on foot on the long trek to London and, after waiting outside his mansion for three days, delivered a petition to the Duke of Argyll, in his capacity as commissioner for Scotland.

Impressed by Helen's devotion to her sister, the Duke delivered the petition to George II who, also moved by her heartfelt plea to save her sister's life, granted a pardon.

Isabella's life was saved and she subsequently married, while Helen, her saviour, died about 1791 and was buried in Irongray churchyard.

In the world of the sciences, John Walker, born in Edinburgh in 1730, was the schoolmaster's son who, after obtaining a degree in divinity in 1749 and being ordained into the Church of Scotland, spent his spare time immersed in the study of chemistry and mineralogy.

Touring the Highlands and Hebridean islands in periods between 1764 and 1771, the erstwhile minister made an exhaustive study of plants, minerals, animals, and climate.

His skills as a gifted naturalist were recognised by the scientific community in 1779 when he was appointed to the prestigious chair of professor of natural history at Edinburgh University, a post he held until his death in 1803.

Another John Walker, born in Stockton-on-Tees in 1781, also achieved scientific fame (and the gratitude of generations of smokers), when he invented the friction match by mixing potash and antimony.

Born in Scranton, Pennsylvania, in 1937, John Anthony Walker is the former chief warrant officer and communications specialist for the U.S. Navy who sold vital secrets to the Soviet Union from 1968 to 1985.

Walker, who has the dubious distinction of being one of the most effective and destructive Soviet spies in U.S. history, was convicted of espionage and received multiple prison sentences.

A rather more popular contemporary figure is Murray Walker, the former British motor sport commentator who was born in Birmingham in 1923, and who commentated on Formula One from the 1950s until 2001.

Internationally popular is the famous Johnnie Walker brand of whisky, first known as Walker's Kilmarnock Whisky, and first blended in the Ayrshire town in the 1820s by John Walker.